G000254731

Lookout

Poetry from Aldeburgh Beach

The Lookout Tower (2010) by Tessa Newcomb

Lookout

Poetry from Aldeburgh Beach

edited by Tamar Yoseloff

Lookout
editions

First published November 2016 by Lookout Editions
31 Crag Path, Aldeburgh, Suffolk IP15 5BS

ISBN 978 0 9956250 0 6

© Lookout Editions 2016
Frontmatter texts, poems and statements © the authors 2016

The moral rights of the authors are asserted in accordance with the
Copyright, Designs and Patents Act 1988. All rights reserved. No
part of this book may be reproduced or utilised, in any form or by
any means, electronic or mechanical, without permission in writing
from the publisher.

A CIP record for this book is available from the British Library

Photographs of pebbles courtesy Fran Crowe
Image on cover and on pp. 12–13 courtesy Eonism/Shutterstock.com

Design and typesetting by Andrew Lindesay
at the Golden Cockerel Press, London

Fonts: Almaq Rough by Dalton Maag and FF Spinoza
Printed and bound by T.J. International Ltd, Padstow, Cornwall

Contents

Foreword

by Grey Gowrie

Francis Carnwath and Caroline Wiseman honour the great Aldeburgh musical tradition established by Benjamin Britten and Peter Pears through emulation. They want to extend it to the written and visual arts. If I were the mayor of Salzburg, I'd hire them to liberate that city, if only a little, from the glory of Mozart in the same way. The Lookout – the tower and the anthology – celebrate their work in progress.

You cannot look at the photograph on the cover without thinking of Tennyson's line, altogether Aldeburghian, "Break, break, break,/ On thy cold grey stones, O Sea!". Tennyson was born and raised further up the North Sea coastline, in Lincolnshire. His father, the Rev. George, would drive a selection of his ten children, Alfred among them, in a pony and trap to Skegness, a place today that forms an Alan Ayckbourn rather than a Ben Britten world. Rows of immobile mobile homes gaze at a marine forest of wind turbines. I happen to find Skeggie visually compelling, but dull would we be of eye not to rejoice in Aldeburgh's long boulevard by its beach of cold grey stones.

So this beach anthology is well named. The North German and Scandinavian tribes who settled in East Anglia, fighting and mating with each other and with the Romano-Celtic peoples they found here, did establish the great poetic tradition we call Anglo-Saxon. I have always found it odd that in the second and third centuries after Christ, a settled and quite prosperous Romano-British civilisation seems bereft of decent poetry (you have to turn to A. E. Housman or Charles Williams or David Jones to find some inventions). But the Anglo-Saxons, who arrived here later, revered the sea they had crossed. "Swan's way" and "whale's road" are among their coinages. "Tanker lane" or "container crossing" might be among ours. This stretch of the North Sea is among the two or three busiest industrial waterways of the world.

Lookout editor Tamar Yoseloff assembles poets who celebrate and gain benefit from the tower itself and even more from its prospect. The sea is both metaphor and actuality. Life on our planet derives from the sea and is sustained by the sun's ability to obliterate salt through condensation as well as the moon's magnetic engine. This book is shot through with bullets of perception by poets I know and read often as well as those new to me. I am going to stand it beside one of my favourite critical studies: W. H. Auden's *The Enchafèd Flood: Or The Romantic Iconography of the Sea*. Auden analyses the late 18th-century shift of style and sensibility which we call Romanticism by considering how its exemplars treated the sea. From Homer to the Romantics it was mainly a dangerous nuisance. Compare Dryden's or Pope's indifference with Wordsworth's echoing seashell found in the middle of a desert in *The Prelude* or Arnold's "melancholy, long, withdrawing roar" of religion in 'Dover Beach'. As a child, Charles Darwin was perplexed and inspired by finding marine fossils high up in the Shropshire hills. For myself, I square the blue planet's watery circle by staying with Eliot's "The sea has many voices./ Many gods and many voices". You will find some of them here.

Preface

by Caroline Wiseman

The Lookout is magical. Tessa Newcomb, in her painting we reproduce as the frontispiece to this book, shows me swimming in the sea lost in a reverie just after I had first set eyes on this fairy-tale tower on Aldeburgh beach. As I swam, I envisioned it as a place of inspiration for artists, poets, writers and musicians from all around the world.

As Blake Morrison describes the Lookout: "It's perfectly situated between town and sea, beach and sky, people and solitude..." This is the same beach where Benjamin Britten walked every day composing music in his head. Since that morning six years ago when I first saw it, the Lookout has been a catalyst for hundreds (almost) to express their creativity in their unique and surprising ways.

Poetry was new to me then, but not to my partner and co-conspirator, Francis Carnwath. He and Grey Gowrie, as school boys together, recited poetry most days. Art has been my passion, but as an art dealer my artists were usually dead; I was never close to the creative process. But now, each day I am up close to the shock of creativity, the endlessly fascinating phenomenon which makes us human.

Interestingly, our last exhibition in London before settling in Aldeburgh was 'Double Visions'. *The London Magazine* had asked me if some of their poets could respond to our artists. So Annie Freud chose a drawing of her grandmother by her father Lucian. George Szirtes chose a Hodgkin, Robert Vas Dias a Pasmore, and so on; they have since visited us here and are included in this anthology. There is, of course, a long history of artists and poets coming together. Matisse/Ronsard, for example, or Picasso/Góngora — I have sold their works over the years. The tradition continues at the Lookout. Poet Harriet Tarlo and artist Judith Tucker worked as a duo; poet Leanne Moden, artist Fran Crowe and composer Nathan Williamson jointly presented 'The Museum of Beyond'. Ian McMillan's 'The John Cage Egg' relates to our 840 eggs, each hand-painted by the artist Liza Adamczewski and then boiled for 4 minutes 33 seconds precisely for the performance of Satie's *Vexations*, which we repeated 840 times as part of Cage's Musicircus for the Aldeburgh Festival in 2014.

Leaking roof, no central heating, camp bed... Julia Bird invited six poets to each spend a night alone in the tower. All were stoical, but I remember in particular the huge relief I felt when Simon Barraclough emerged alive from the tower one freezing February morning after witnessing the sunrise. His poem is one of my favourites.

Poets love the bleak beauty of Aldeburgh beach — indeed the important poet Herbert Lomas lived and died opposite the Lookout, in the house next door to us. Poets love it so much that they are holding their very own festival, 'Poetry in Aldeburgh', which will be the perfect occasion to launch this wonderful anthology. My huge thanks to Tamar Yoseloff for suggesting it and then editing it with such passion and professionalism.

Introduction

by Tamar Yoseloff

It's been my privilege to assemble this book, as one of the poets who benefitted from a Lookout residency — thanks to the generosity of Caroline Wiseman and Francis Carnwath — but also as a lover of Aldeburgh. You can't help but hear the first orchestral interlude from Britten's *Peter Grimes*, the high gull cry of the violins, as you walk along the beach. Maggi Hambling celebrates that extraordinary conflation of music and landscape in her tribute to Britten, her sculpture *Scallop* that resides on the shingle, between sea and town. Incised in its steel ridges are Britten's words: *I hear those voices that will not be drowned.*

Nor will the voices in this anthology. We've brought together 32 poets, who have come to Aldeburgh by Caroline's invitation, or through the annual Aldeburgh Poetry Festival, or who have had deep roots in the place for some time. All share a love of Aldeburgh, and have found the words to express it, in poems and accounts. What Caroline has created is a refuge for artists, film-makers, writers and musicians to ruminate on the landscape. For those who've slept in the Lookout, with nothing more than a fire in the grate and a camp bed, it's provided access to the sea and its mysterious movements. One of the strongest memories of my Lookout experience is waking in the night to hear the sound of the waves breaking on the pebbles then dragging them back, their regular reach and pull lulling me again to sleep.

Poets always have stories behind their poems, and we've gathered some good ones. Simon Barraclough's near-death experience. Tim Cumming's fish supper. Anna Selby's strange dreams. The 'hour in the tower', a quick-fire poem challenge sponsored by the poetry festival and cheerfully accepted by Matthew Caley, Rody Gorman and Penelope Shuttle. The meeting of image and word: John Craske's threads weaving into Rebecca Farmer's poems; Bill Jackson's night vision enlightening Sue Rose; Fran Crowe's beachcombings fuelling both Ian McMillan and Leanne Moden; George Szirtes and Robert Vas Dias channelling Howard Hodgkin; Harriet Tarlo and Judith Tucker's seafront walking each dawn and dusk; Gerry Loose and Morven Gregor shaping nature into poems and photographs; Michael Horovitz and Vanessa Vie sending exuberant songs into the air. There are strange things on the horizon: Claire Crowther's sighting of Sizewell B, Siriol Troup's Martello Tower. Some poets know this coast intimately, and write from the vantage point of many years of trawling the shoreline: Daphne Astor, Anne Berkeley, Pamela Johnson, Anne-Marie Fyfe, Andrea Porter, Blake Morrison, Annie Freud, Catherine Coldstream, Ian Griffiths. Several braved challenging winter weather: Rebecca Perry, Julia Bird, Joey Connolly and Gemma Seltzer.

From the top of the tower, you have a clear view of squalls and storms, spectacular cloudscapes, doom-laden greys. But this project has been all blue skies and bright sun. I'd like to thank the poets who have shared their work; Andrew Lindesay for his beautiful book design; Humphrey Burton, Liz Calder, Libby Purves and Roger Wright for their enthusiastic endorsements; Grey Gowrie for his wonderful Foreword; and of course, Francis and Caroline for their vibrant support and nurturing of the arts. This book is a tribute to their vision.

Daphne Astor

I write poetry alone but in my artwork I have been collaborating with Ermias Kifleyesus since 2004 and our collaborative residency at the Lookout in 2014 was called AS IT IS. During one week we made work in many different mediums with a narrative focus on Aldeburgh, Southwold, Dunwich and Sizewell. In the top Lookout room we created an installation of silhouettes portraying historical and contemporary Aldeburgh people, animals, buildings and plants through which you could see the sky, sea, shingle and the town itself – this was accompanied by a sound piece with Aldeburgh noises, borrowed texts and readings of poetry by George Crabbe and others. In the middle room we showed an installation of smoked sprats, a portrait and small film of local master embroiderer Kirsten Hecktermann creating a silk sprat on velvet. In the downstairs room we hung collages, paintings and large pencil drawings of heroic fishermen based on photographs we sourced from the Southwold Sailors' Reading Room. At night we projected films onto the exterior of the Lookout tower that we had shot at dawn on Dunwich beach, picturing the incoming tide as it washed away drawings and writings we had imposed on each other's skin.

For both of us, our residency was an intense week with total focus on hunting and gathering inspiration around Suffolk then returning to the Lookout with ideas from which we made the art. It was an honour that Caroline Wiseman and Francis Carnwath included us in the eclectic collection of contemporary residencies at the tower. My poem 'Looking Out' was written in 2016 during a storm while I sheltered against an outside wall of the Lookout.

Looking Out

Passing together through the months of our slow courtship
we had occasion to study the philosophy of beginnings
by recollecting the energy which had spurred us forward —

concerning your private life I never liked to ask questions
as I knew that for some unknown reason the moon
had not been seen the night before the half naked sailors

rowed us down river. On our wedding morning under a low cool sun
we shared a delicious cup of tea on the veranda of your house
where the air was scented by rain bruised white rose petals and

where presently a person came into your garden — who he was
and why he called we shall never know — but he said
after all you are only playing at being nomads.

Anne Berkeley

I have been privileged to visit Aldeburgh each November since the 1990s, for the Aldeburgh Poetry Festival. I usually stay in a cottage near the beach to watch the fishermen and search for hag stones and things that the sea throws up. There is satisfaction in ploughing through the pebbles, sometimes arranging them to make a pattern for the sea to destroy, sometimes looking to the horizon and thinking of Europe, sometimes just staring at the sea in deliberate self-forgetfulness. My poem arose from a workshop at the festival where painters and writers each tried the other's discipline.

The painters are drawing the sea

The painters are drawing the sea.
They pour themselves into it endlessly.

Norma is collaging the sea: scraps of old paper, old news.
Frances is cross-hatching the sea on a sketch-pad.
Ian is thumbing the sea in charcoal, the sea blackening his thumb.
Joanna is staring into the sea.
Dean is thinking about the sea, adding to it with a few strokes of the pen.
Honor is laying the sea on with a palette knife, scooping up its
     bluey greys and stroking: now sea, now rain, now curtains.
And she is putting a frame round the sea.
David is swaying in time to the sea.
Roy is at an angle to the sea, washing and writing in it.

I cannot draw. At the foam's edge, I let the sea rush over my hand.

Simon Barraclough

I stayed at the Lookout tower one freezing-cold night in February after a day of constant snowfall and long traffic jams. Caroline and Francis took me out for a warming dinner, with plenty of red wine, and I took a midnight walk on the beach, listening to the new My Bloody Valentine album through my headphones and taking murky, abstract photos of the foamy breakers with my low-quality phone camera. I met a man walking his dog and that encounter gave me the title of the poem. I returned to the Lookout and lit the fire to try and keep warm. I got all my bedding together and scribbled some notes with stiff, cold, painful fingers. I then fell asleep on top of my bedding instead of under it and when I awoke at 5am. I didn't know where I was or who I was and I was in so much pain from the cold that, for a few seconds, I genuinely thought that I had died and been sent to an icy circle of Hell. I couldn't move. In the end, I stirred and climbed the tower to watch a muted, reluctant sunrise. I'm pleased with the poem I wrote and pleased to be alive.

On the Care and Handling of Seas

There are many different sizes and shapes of sea.
Try to pick one that suits your home and lifestyle.
If you own or are responsible for a sea,
even for a short while,
you are required by law to take proper care of it.
Seas are active and need three meals a day.
A well-balanced diet of protein, carbohydrate, fats, vitamins, and
    minerals is recommended.
Water should be provided with meals and after exercise.
By one hundred thousand years, a sea is ready for obedience training.

During training, the sea should never be struck with the hand or any
    other object.
The word 'No' should be used in a firm and authoritative manner.
The sea should first be taught to heel.
Once the sea has mastered heeling, it can be taught to sit.
It can then be taught to stay.
It may choose to fetch of its own free will.
A sea's surface requires grooming to keep it healthy and clean.
A sea should not be bathed frequently since baths remove essential oils.
The sea's teeth should be scrubbed periodically with a small toothbrush.
Grinding tectonic plates into pebbles may help with dental hygiene.

Outdoor seas need a protective shelter, like a cave or cove.
A sea needs a bed to retreat to when it is tired or sick.
Seas are sociable and mix well with other bodies of water.
They are subject to monthly bouts of lunacy.
Some more than others.
Be on the lookout
for mood swings, a dreamy expression, impossible pregnancies.
The Dead Sea is a misnomer
but if your sea has not moved for a very long time
it may, in fact, have died.

Julia Bird

Packing to sleep out in the Lookout on a February night? Here's what you need: two pairs of pyjama bottoms, three pairs of socks, two jumpers, a cardigan, gloves, a woolly hat, a scarf, a sleeping bag, a duvet, five blankets and a fur coat to go over the top. Sweet dreams...

The Boast

As a girl, I won badges for this skill:
    campfires lit with pages of *The Wilts & Glos,*
a ration of leaf-mould and a single match.
    A firelighter is a little cube of poison fudge.
Even now, from a pile of pigeon moult,
    a rasping Zippo and a damp receipt,
I can spark it up. I'll kindle you a blaze
    that frees the sun-flare trapped inside a pine's
heart-wood; a snapping, spitting fire
    that draws up a chimney like a fervent prayer,
a fire that stirs a room's whole air
    to heat haze, that shows itself in miniature
in glass and metal, skin and porcelain, a fire
    that warms you through but scorches in a second
any letter you may choose to burn.
    In the morning, when you think the hearth is dead,
I'll find the dull red sweeties in the ash
    and, with a twist of paper handkerchief
and whispered streams of coaxing spells,
    will breed a bed of yellow crocus flames.
Yellow dancing girls. Orange soldiers
    who will follow any orders that I make.
When we've charred our way through every forest,
    torched our chopped up chairs and kicked in doors;
when all that's left to warm up in the embers
    is crab-apples and stones, you may call me on this boast.

Matthew Caley

The Aldeburgh Poetry Festival works you hard (in a good way) — a reading with Don Paterson and J O Morgan, a workshop, a talk on 'poetic thievery' — and late nights at DP's (my fault; the only vaguely disreputable pub I could find along the main drag). Spilling beer all over myself with the inestimable Peter Blegvad talking Pataphysics and The Golden Palominos. So a stint in this folly was blissful rest. Touch of vertigo up the ladder, then I'm left to it. I never even attempted the poem I was supposed to write there — my writing process (if it might be called that) rarely touches on direct description and it's hard to write to order — would only mention the sea if I was inland — and indeed the extract from 'The Foldings' here — one stanza from a long poem — was written in the Czech Republic. But the time up aloft was great — very tranquil and contemplative, my faint hangover and the sea-haze/sky-haze staring each other out. So it was quite an interruption (in a good way) when someone came to interview me for the festival podcast and I had to come up with something coherent about the experience. Then another when the unwaveringly cheerful Luke Kennard bounded up the ladder to relieve me of my watch. But I often make my way now to Trinity Buoy Wharf in East India Docks, across the river from the Millennium Dome, to stand in the bulb of the lighthouse, looking at seagulls and cable cars and listening to Jem Finer's art installation 'Longplayer' — a piece with music made by singing bowls and computers that is playing for a thousand years — which seems very much a parallel experience — so maybe the time in the Lookout seeped in after all.

from **The Foldings**

     The fishermen strain
together to haul in the
bell-buoys, this hammock
made of former   broken nets
is slung between   *air*   and   *air*
diamonds of air-weave
held fast by taut tackle-blocks
gull's cries   or children's
such verisimilitude
to everything that is freed

       sky like *Tuinal*
tremor of the basking shark
sleep is a thick book
binding blue   the shallows clear
the deep   trawlerman's turquoise

Catherine Coldstream

My time at the Lookout was intense and windswept. An early April, the gulls and rain were my companions as I sat and wrote in the tower, or in the beautiful setting of Caroline Wiseman's seafront home in Crag Path. The long days swung between morning walks on sand and pebble, and the warmth of evening meals around Caroline and Francis's deliciously well-stocked table.

Taking time out of a busy teaching schedule to write, compose, and reflect on the personal influence of my father, the painter William Coldstream, was an extraordinary privilege. The space afforded by the Lookout — cold and desolate though it felt at times — was exactly what I needed to work on my material, weaving words, music and film footage into a multimedia installation that incorporated elements of the Suffolk coast. Only in such an uncluttered and liminal space could I have felt so free.

Shoreline

I am steeple bright, yet swathed in shadows.

By the shoreline you appear —
a fullness fading

and somewhere, a bell
that began to ring
one summer — one late June
when we drank saké on a balcony
in the suburbs of a small industrial town in Germany —
can be heard again, dancing
in the twilight with the elves
that live on the outskirts of the forest.

Before the fullness fades
I hear it softly
under the trees —

that bell.

Joey Connolly

remember arriving in Aldeburgh, and at the Lookout, then wondering immediately about what it meant to arrive at a place and then try and find words for that place — that's what I felt like it was my job to do there. But the wondering took up all the space, and the thing I was supposed to be wondering about took a few steps back. I spent my days trying to balance the scales between the Aldeburgh coast and my trying to pay attention to the Aldeburgh coast. I spent time in the pub, and back in the Lookout, eating fish and chips while staring at blank but increasingly grease-stained pieces of paper. Eventually I fell back into simple lists of the things I could see — the lights of tankers, triangles of seagulls, tortoiseshell-colour shingle — the things that definitely seemed outside of me. So when I came to write about them, I found myself writing a lot about vision and about looking. And I wrote about arriving into a place, and how that's like arriving into a set of new words (oh boy, poets...) — I suppose the words of people who've been in places like this before you. Taken in again.

Themselves

I have learned the words — curlicue,
arabesque, craquelure — and I have done my best
to feel that well-spoken weft &c. beneath
the skin of things, with ketamines or caffeines
mingling with the bloodstream I have long
been shifting, twice changing between Liverpool Street,
between St Pancras and here. All preparation
dissolves like cardboard-minded
hangover morning vitamin supplement at this
sudden coast, the mist-hung edges of this shingle beach,
its pitchless singing, its pebble-rattle intensifying
to the static hiss of unthinkable numbers, this
vast variegate of stone being
dragged across itself by the persistent
knowing drugged retreat
of the waves, and the gentle waves — patina, spindrift,
astringent — and the waves. The vast multiplication table
of its rattle. The mingling of the symbols for stones
with the symbol for seawater rinsing the two,
the three-inch give of a tortoiseshell of shingle
underfoot, the way every rounded collateral pressure
of stone on deeper stone comes up
through the shoesoles, the soles of the feet,
up through some rail-cartographer's dream of nerves,
up to the neck and the graze there of the salt-air
on the tongue, scouring off the need for words
and, a breath after that, the words

What Must be Tankers

By eight the dark speaks false, freely,
about where the sky
might be meeting the sea. But a line,
a line

of distant lights has taken up the work
instead, pins of a darkish red from what must be
tankers, anchored offshore, fixing for us
some attenuated idea

of horizon. Perhaps twenty; they flute
and flicker. They wane,
and then again assert themselves,
little vermillion self-effacements
against the dark, the dispirited survivors of daylight's
failed coup.

They brighten and fade, as if
so-many minor generals were
gathered and dragging
urgently on expensive final cigars
before the firing squad or as if
the record button on some inexplicable host of tape-decks
were all improperly depressed and only half
of everything .

were being taken in. Yes can the
persistent inconstancy of those
scarlet pins be right, or do my eyes
play tricks? No, must I remind myself
that eyes

do not play tricks?, that light is a trick. The process
of vision an unspeakably capable magician's
grand finale, an unspeakable sleight of hand, one thing
exchanged incredibly for another, the dry
colourless sand of particles and packs of strings swapped
invisibly for

the rich inescapable pictures we are
provided with and are, and we are
taken in. Particles and waves, the shipping
and docking of data, the vague freight
of sense, the flipped lighthouse-beam of sight,
the pointillist pinprick-stock of grain that light holds
in the dark galley of itself

like a cargo, fluctuating
in value and clarity and the sea
always offering up its deep endless stirring.
It's cold here on the beach but it sounds of warmth, like waves of
significance and contentedness
and I, entirely, am entirely taken in.

Claire Crowther

cientific achievement is made visible at Aldeburgh, that most reflective of seaside resorts. On my first visit, I sat on the beach enjoying the stones and then strolled towards Southwold. It was a clear day. The pressurized water nuclear reactor, Sizewell B, loomed up. And there on the right, in the sea, and distant, spread the beneficent arms of a wind power array. Since then, on Aldeburgh beach, I've often thought over these giants of power. The Lookout allows distance, mood and decision to work together for an artist. And for a scientist. The two forms of discovery have much in common and I'm currently writing a sequence of poems about the practice of solar science.

Solar Science Imagined as a Refuge

The sun is his job.
He stays out longer than the family want,

upstairs in the Lookout.
We think he meets someone there we don't know.

Once he touched a photo
of our wedding — the two of us, him,

me. With his ring finger,
he traced the image of my face.

Then he traced his own face.
I spend nights wondering

about unlikeliness,
his singular tasks, his research, his remit.

He brings me discoveries:
the strain balance quantum well solar cell.

The Lookout keeps him late,
pulling the energy of waves to us.

Tim Cumming

As brief poetic residencies go, it was a pretty good fish supper. I read while the artists ate. A table of visual artists with visual wealth, compared to the relatively pauper poets with an incomplete grant application. A big fella who earned his wealth from the brush turned to me and said, "You're a poet? Poor bugger. You must be starving."

Up the ladder of the Lookout, I tussled a little with the resident vertigo, and settled on the creaking boards to stare out to sea, up to sky. The sky is bigger than a blank canvas here, bigger than the white sheet a poet fills or covers the body with. The sky is a body of work, and I opened my Cloud Book, and wrote.

Cloud Book

Above us we observe how
clouds break and gather.
It bears no familiar, no easy
likening to our own behaviour,
way downstream and moving
together, straining ourselves
through one day then another
and dissolving our condition
as clouds break and gather
way up there beyond our reach.
Look at them!
For size and scale they eclipse
everything we do beneath.
We are not to scale.
When we are in love
we are not to scale.
Parts of us are much too large
to fit comfortably
into our mysterious skin,
the body's organ of first contact.
See how it forms in the womb,
like folds of cumulus.
To use this cloud book,
supply a room, and rub in gently,
then with vigour, as light
turns to dark in each corner,
the sky at the window a pale
tattered net dragging up stars
to set across our table at dusk.

Sehnsucht

After you have gone I want you
to show me once again with your
mouth, how you hold and shape
that word for unfathomable longing,
sehnsucht, the way it breaks
upon your lips, releasing the pressure
at its centre and within that,
your roaming profile, memory,
of all the unfathomable longings,
the way you carry it in yourself,
that word in your throat,
not daring to break it but
breaking it open all the same;
now bring it to your lips and say it.

Celebrate the
pebbles
forever, look

leave nothing but a
sea-salted teaspoon.

Why are there stones
on the beach?
Felix ☺

Rebecca Farmer

I n June 2015 I spent a week at the Lookout tower working with the artist Katharine Fry. Our work took the form of a conversation conducted against the soundscape of that overwhelming and continuous conversation between the sea and the land. Aldeburgh is a place full of inspirations and staircases. When I climbed the staircase to the Peter Pears Gallery I found they were packing away an exhibition of embroideries by the Norfolk fisherman John Craske (1881–1943). I use poems as other people might use photographs and I wanted to try to hang on to his wonderful work — even as it disappeared into the bubble wrap.

On Witnessing the Dismantling of the
John Craske Exhibition at Aldeburgh

Two women arrive to pack away the sea.
They are armed with bubble wrap.
I must be quick to photograph

the tilting ships, the apricot sails,
figures battling against his limitless sea
in gales so real they knock the breath out of me.

The herrings made in a running stitch
smell of fish, their silvers and blues
catch the light and wink at me.

I no longer see where sky ends
and sea begins; water laps at my feet
like a labrador's lick.

Grey clouds shift, darkness falls,
a lighthouse beam shines from the wall;
with Christ in the vessel we'll smile at the storm.

The current is too strong, I have to give in
like the dancing fishermen
who never learnt to swim.

When the two women find me
they'll think I'm asleep,
bound in seaweed-coloured threads that reek of iodine.

Annie Freud

I spent much of my childhood in Walberswick, a coastal village a few miles away from Aldeburgh, as my paternal grandparents, about whom this poem was written, had a house there called Hidden House after Hiddensee, an island in the Baltic where they had spent the summer holiday with their children before leaving Germany for Britain in 1933. They did things differently from everyone else. Their food was rich and saucy. Like many Germans, my grandfather knew about mushrooms, where to find them and how to cook them. My grandparents slept under continental quilts, unheard-of in those days. I adored my grandmother. All her possessions had a kind of fastidious stylishness — her pruning scissors, her outfits, her china and the methods she used to carry out her household tasks were also very particular. My grandparents spoke and thought differently from other people. They were foreign.

I have recently made a painting of the house on Hiddensee from a small photograph taken by her. All my feelings of love for her, and my sense of the terrible wrench that leaving such a beloved place must have been for her, are in that painting.

Head of a Woman

I remember the mornings before Pap died
long before I'd heard of things like suicide,
the teacups sprigged with dark blue flowers,
your Chinese robe embroidered with towers,
peonies, dragons and battling cranes,
rubbing Windolene on the window panes,
your Beethoven hairdo striped like a badger's,
the coat you bought me from Swan and Edgar's,
my Milky Way sliced wafer thin,
the satiny texture of your skin,
the way you said *parsley* and *sickening brute*
with the R rolled and the U drawn out,
the kisses you blew me from your fingertips,
magnificent old person, my perfectionist.

Anne-Marie Fyfe

A real gift to spend time at the South Lookout tower in a late-autumn week: to spend each day on a mesmerising water's edge, in shifting East Coast light. My days there took me back to roots, in Ireland, where I grew up just yards from the Sea of Moyle, the quick-tempered strait between Ireland and Scotland. My first poetry publication was a chapbook titled 'A House by the Sea', and in one poem, I find myself asking what brings me back, year after year, to that particular sea-girt world. Aldeburgh's Lookout residency certainly brought me back, as any coastal sojourn unfailingly does, to my own coastal margins and shorelines and tidal pull. What's different about Aldeburgh is the quality of light, constantly changing from dawn to sunset, to innumerable shades of dusk and darkness. And always that horizon hazily observed from the tower's watch-room, at the top of a winding stair. I loved watching the changing tides, on misty or sharply sunlit mornings, almost as much as I enjoyed weathering the nostalgic rattle of November rain on the tower's roof and sea spray on the bolted boathouse doors. Strange, then, to come back in dead of winter to London's sheltering terraces, to less vivid light, less insistent rain-sounds, and the sudden absence of sea, but with so much of that other world captured and condensed into drafts that, with each distant tide, creep closer to being an account, a response in words, to the experience of living on such edges, a sequence that like so many works of art would not exist without the determined commitment of sponsors such as the visionary Caroline Wiseman.

Shoreline

The high sea-wall, a beach-hut's paint-blister, four cormorants,
oars and floats, the sadness of a deflated beach ball,

fish-scales clustering like my kid brother's stamp hinges,
rock-crusted limpets with slimy insides,

a pinch of sand in un-salty tomato sandwiches,
buckets without spades, the rubberiness of kelp,

limestone headlands, ex-Navy binoculars, a pink-petalled bathing cap,
bamboo fishing net, conical shells, perfect skimming-stones,

our car reversing close to a pier's edge, a stench of lugworm,
July sandcastles that were always too wet, too dry,

the cancelled Sunday Regatta, the clarity of Limerick Point rockpools.

On the Slipway

A gutting-knife's moon-glistened blade,
cable-stitch of John Roy's nubbly gansey,
the shudder on first looking at a dogfish,

eerily giant footprints in wet sand,
cooling slap of calamine lotion after sunshine,
my uncle's accordion shanties from a darkening porch,

dip and pull of each oar in serious waters,
the stark white of our house from this side of the point,
that homecoming judder as a keel grates on beachstones once again.

Rody Gorman

What I remember most about participating at the Aldeburgh Poetry Festival was the warm and enthusiastic reception for my own work and that of the other participating poets from Scottish islands, showing what an inclusive event the festival is.

Tùr ann an Aldeburgh

Agus mi ri mo dhàn
Gu h-àrd anns an tùr
Leam fhìn fad uair a thìde,

Chì mi sa mhol cailleach
Bhuam agus clann-nighean
Shìos air an dà ghlùin

Is maide 'n làmh gach duine
'S iad a' cur rin saothair fhèin
Mar gun robh iad san tràigh-mhaorach

Sna faochagan anns an eilean
Seach an tòir air an òr
Fodhpa 's cnàmhan Bhritten.

Earthmindsensetower in Aldeburgh

As I'm working away at my fatepoem up there in that
earthmindsensetower of mine on my own for an hour of the
tideclock, I see in the praiseflockshingle a nunhag and young
girls down on both generationknees and every manone of them
has a stick in their hand as they work away at their own tidal-
islandlabours as if they were down at the eddyeyewhelks on
the shore back in the island and not toryafter the gold beneath
them and Britten's bones.

Ian Griffiths

Aldeburgh has long been recognised as a focus for the arts in East Anglia, in particular the music festival founded by Benjamin Britten. It has also become home to a poetry festival and is a centre for notable art and craft exhibitions reflecting the diverse talent of our region.

How very appropriate and what a blessing it has been then that Caroline Wiseman should have moved to Aldeburgh, purchased the South Lookout on the beach, and set up her Arts Club which brings together the creative minds of the region. The Lookout itself is an appropriate icon, representing an attitude of outward looking. It provides a hub of artistic networking which reaches worldwide.

As a poet who trained originally as an artist, I am full of enthusiasm for the various art forms working together. It is more important than ever in these difficult times for arts funding that creatives should work together and maximise their resources to mutual benefit. Artists often work alone but the opportunity afforded by Caroline's enterprise to share ideas is both stimulating and nourishing. I am most grateful to Caroline and Francis for affording the poets of the Suffolk Poetry Society the use of the Lookout on National Poetry Day. I was pleased to read my poem 'The Light Keeper's Daughter' from the top of the Lookout steps, a poem which referenced the NPD's theme of light. And what more appropriate location and backdrop could there have been, with the gulls crying overhead.

Caroline's Lookout is on our country's eastern edge, and the work you will find represented there will often have an edge, embrace technology wherever appropriate, and be outward-looking. I am honoured to be part of it.

The Light Keeper's Daughter

An early evening light
washed low across the table
as our hands dipped to the pail
side by side,
the warm glow of evening
setting fire to our cheeks.

Occasionally and almost imperceptibly
our hands brushed,
clutched the rough skin spuds,
soil falling away between our fingers,
discovering their forms,
we stripped and lay them
smooth, naked, pale, wet,
revealed upon the kitchen counter

And how it came to be I can't recall
but that evening we walked together
up the cliff side path,
the sea resounding on the rocks below,
air thick with kittiwake and gull cry,
shearwaters hurling themselves
into the night to feed far out
upon the swelling breast of the Atlantic.

Together in the lamp-black night,
interrogated only by the sweep of lighthouse beam,
we had no use of words
for I felt your warmth calling me
against the heather of the hill
and without direction our hands met
fingers linked palm met palm.

We turned and as we drew each other close
twin beams of unforgiving light
flung our shadows out into the screaming dark.
Two ghosted children,
hands hung limply at our sides
for whom five years might pass
for such a time to come again.

But somewhere on that cliff path
there is a moment that still hangs upon the air —
he did not come to take me home.
We embraced and lifted to the wind
and with shearwater kittiwake and gull
inclined our faces to the sky
and with one voice
let forth a great and raucous cry.

PEBBLE DASHED

I AM ONE
IN A
MILLION

Dieti
be a
ming

have fun!

THE NE
16.05.1

Michael Horovitz
& Vanessa Vie

Looking back at Aldeburgh: *in August 2013 we were invited by Caroline Wiseman to spend three days in Aldeburgh, exhibiting our visual work in her Art House on Crag Path, and performing music and poetry in her groundbreaking Lookout tower, which surges magisterial on the strand facing the gallery.*

The party was on. Bleached pebble beach, zigzagging sun on windsurfing waves, horizon line picturesquely broken by a scattering of boat-sails; Caroline's lavish tables spread with sea food and delicatessen and refreshing white wines; public afternoon performances outside the Tower — an enigmatic height up its spiral staircase each artist is invited to climb and bear witness. Vanessa wrote in her notebook there: "What I think? — I don't know. What I see? — the Sea. What do I say this is? — Power, in the eye of the beholder."

Evening performances inside the Tower's ground-base were candle-lit, recalling folkloric essence of coastal neighbourhoods and associations.

Aldeburgh's Carnival is a popular local event (next year will mark its 75th anniversary). We were lucky our sojourn with Caroline coincided with this community celebration. Young boys and girls, extended families, all manner of performers and writers, barbecues, parades, fireworks, multi-style dancing, and to cherry our memory, a fabulous full moon roundelay.

On the morning of our departure back south, Caroline's gallery assistant invited us out to see the sun rising whilst bathing in the mercurial 5am Suffolk sea. Rebellious clouds were sailing up ahoy, and the sun rose behind them. The water was cold and the beach deserted. The Lookout beckoned, familiar landmark to return to from meditative shoreward walks.

Francis Carnwath, Caroline's partner of many years, inconspicuously charmed our mega-creative days and nights with insightful conversation and consistent good humours. Francis drove us back to the train station, somewhat bemused by the volume of our luggage — not only jam-packed suitcases, but all of our framed and unframed artworks, musical instruments, et al.

How we managed to get all the way to Aldeburgh and then back again to London, frolicking oblivious to our physical strain, we still hardly know. Perhaps it was that Caroline's Aldeburgh set-up harmonises so well with our own socio-artistic aspirations.

Sea Song
(by Michael Horovitz)

Lips part   *breaking*
　　shored bowstring   *ebbing*
　arrows －   echoes
of violin gut   *flowing*
　　to the conductor's
　　　fingertip command
then snapping
　　mouth
　　　opens   wide   *breaking*
its tongue
　　barks －   foams   *ebbing*
　　reft of music
　　　babbles bricks
throat spews   *flowing*
　　　old newsreels
drunken toasts
　　on boats and tides   *breaking*
　　　high ideals   *ebbing*
with dynasties
　　flags   － great quests
　　　loves and deaths
long forgot
　　battle spoils   *flowing*
　　　banquet dregs   *breaking*
broken teeth
　　images －   all   *ebbing*
　　　dream images
　　of listening
　　　without taste
or purpose   *flowing*
　　　－ see
the singing
　　waves   *breaking*
through －   eyes
　　closed
　　　to sound   *ebbing*
on silence －   *flowing*
　　echoes －   arrows －   *breaking*
　　　mind
　　　　　open －

Accordion haiku
(by Vanessa Vie)

Sound of an accordion
Flying above the railway
Shadow of a crow

The Sentinel
(by Vanessa Vie and Michael Horovitz)

On the look-out post
Atop the fishmonger's van
A single seagull

...washing

the wind, the sand a
...res. All kidnaps from the
...make of the air...

am
myself
for
he
thought
to
be
all
that
you
had
but
hadn't
he
said
so
many
fathoms
...y

The Aime of the E...

Pebbles, pebbles,
all i see is pebbl...

Molly, 11.

'ife ha...

Masses
of
Crashing
Pebbles
...t   waves

Pamela Johnson

I spend several weeks a year in Aldeburgh. The beach, with its expansive bands of shingle, sea and sky, is like an ever-changing abstract artwork. The sea can shift from brown to green to turquoise, the sky might hang low with dense cloud or become a vaulting clear blue; tides and storms re-sculpt the shingle. It's never the same place yet always the same place. It's a place to clear the mind, to find a space for thought, an ideal place to be refreshed, ready to write. I love the physicality of it: plunging into the waves for an invigorating swim; walking that rare band of sand at low tide, looking for the perfect pebble which you never find. I'm fascinated by the sheer quantity and variety of stones; studied long enough, some of them will suggest a poem.

The Lookout is a creative meeting place where I enjoy exhibitions, poetry readings, Art Club gatherings: eating, talking about art and poetry with the wind blowing and the sea crashing outside. Magic.

This Pebble

is grey, smooth and matt, it sits
in your palm, snug up to your thumb
wafer flat   this pebble is the colour of the suit
you buried your father in, it's the shape of the birthmark
you hide on your thigh, it's like the sole
of a baby's foot − like the foot of the baby
you lost − or a lozenge that could loosen your tongue
this pebble is the stain on the desk where you spilled
the ink, it's the key to the code that will teach you to read
a beach, could be a comma in a paragraph
of stones or a dying star before it implodes
and becomes a black hole   this pebble is the eye
of the wave devil − stare back and you're sunk   this pebble
wasn't the only one but the one that caught your eye
along miles of shingle, it's flat enough
to skim with a flick of the wrist − watch it bounce
to the curve of the earth − it's a bit of a cliff
that lost its fight with the tide not an obstacle
that will cause you to stumble   this pebble
is the cloud that broke free of the storm
                        yet holds on to its rain

Gerry Loose

he residency at the Lookout was shared with photographer Morven Gregor. Together we researched the coastline, walked many miles and made work specifically related to the area, both visual and textual. We were most particularly taken with Orford Ness: its rare plants, long views and its weapons-testing anomalies (now a rusting, decaying hectares-wide museum). Natural world taking over from humanity's artefacts. Shingle beaches are unknown where we come from in Scotland, so it was a great pleasure to be walking an unusual land (beach) scape and hearing its sounds, seeing its sights. Stones, plants, water effects, like crop sprayers, as well as visions of boats apparently sailing through fields were also strange and vital. Pagodas at Orford! Churches with cool graveyards. So many small sailing craft... and of course the very warm welcome and hospitality of Caroline and Francis.

to
sail
green
meadows

in
heavy
dews

where grass becomes water where becomes fire becomes cloud where

NOTICE

SINCE THERE ARE BLAZES
AND THUNDERHEADS THERE
ARE ALSO FALLS AND ECHOES
SEDGE AND STONECROP
STARWEED AND SPURGE
THE JUSTICE OF SPINDRIFT
WITH BLUE HILLS WALKING
AND CLOUD GATES
FOREVER OPEN
TO REVERIE OF RED SNOW
AND GREEN SUN BESIDE
PEARLWORT AND RIBWORT
WHILE A HARE ON SHINGLE
DAPPLES THE WORLD
AND A FOX IN THE MARSH
PATTERNS US ALL

Ian McMillan

I think that the beach at Aldeburgh and the tower are a kind of poetic paradise, and that if I could choose anywhere for a sudden immersion in the mechanics of inspiration, that place would be it. The moment of climbing the rickety ladder to gaze from the window at the sea is comparable to the moment when a poem begins to resolve itself in your head: there is a flash or clarity, followed by a clamber down to where the real work begins. I worked there with the artist Fran Crowe who taught me so much about the finding of objects and the discarding of nothing as the tide rushed in and out.

Paint and Waves

We are both temporary.
We are both wet.
We are both subject to change.
We are both altering and altering.
We are both permanent. Oh. No, we're not.
We are both the colour of ourselves.
We are both the colour of things we could try to describe but would
     rather not.
We are both difficult to name.
We are both paint and waves at the same time.
We are both waves and paint at the same time.
One of us is waving.
One of us is painting.

It Is

It is as though the sea is geometric,
Washing angled seaweed onto the beach.

It is as though the shadow-tide comes in,
Goes out, leaving shadow-weed, shadow pools.

It is as though sand is a currency that saves itself,
Can never be devalued, especially by seagulls.

It is as though everything is always unfinished,
Waiting for the finishing tide that never arrives.

It is as though the sea is loosened each night,
Tightened each morning, like a soaking scarf.

The John Cage Egg

Now bring to the boil; listen, listen hard
As the bubbles burst suddenly, steam rises

Making silent shapes in the receptive air,
And the egg itself knocks rhythm, rhythms

Against the unthinking pan. The egg hardens
Into the kind of silence you can eat,

The kind of silence you can bring soldiers to,
The kind of silence you can put in, yes, an egg cup

And tap with a spoon. Resonant silence,
The best kind. Turn the egg-timer, slowly:

Boil the egg for exactly 4 minutes, 33 seconds;
No less, no more. Exact, exacting silence.

Leanne Moden

In 2014, I spent a week at the South Lookout for a writer's residency, working on a collection of poems as part of the *Museum of Beyond* project. Designed by Suffolk artist Fran Crowe, the *Museum of Beyond* uses art to draw attention to the vast amount of plastic rubbish currently floating in our oceans. The exhibition itself is set out like a museum, with eroded plastic objects carefully placed behind glass with typed cards explaining how 'Oil Age' people might have used each item. The attention to detail is incredible and, though the artwork is executed with tongue firmly in cheek, the whole thing is really thought-provoking. Aldeburgh beach is such a beautiful part of Britain's coastline, and when juxtaposed against the environmental issues discussed in the *Museum of Beyond* project, it became an incredibly evocative place in which to write.

Lighter

Flick the flint, ignite the spark,
Illuminate the deepest dark.
Illuminate all shades of grey
Until the shadows fade away.
Vanquish every beast and foe,
And light the way you'd wish to go.
Tame the fire and tame yourself,
Search for beauty, not for wealth,
And never compromise your health.
Signal to each passing ship,
Fan the flames and lick your lips.
Turn the wheels and grind the gears
And cauterise your wildest fears.
Take photographs, not souvenirs,
And measure time in days, not years.

Blake Morrison

I've been coming to the East Anglian coast for over 30 years and many of my poems are set there. Though I've never done a residency at the Lookout tower, a couple of my students have and I know the building well: it's perfectly situated between town and sea, beach and sky, people and solitude – a good place both to create work and exhibit it. The sea and shingle of Aldeburgh have inspired writers, artists and musicians for the past two centuries, and will continue to do so in the future.

Flotsam

I remember it like yesterday:
the bell buoy tolling in the rivermouth
and the bodies laid out on the beach.

Their faces flickered in the torchlight
and the buttons on their uniforms
glowed like fire tongs by the hearth.

*

Fire. Or maybe just samphire.
Burning petrol. Or a storm petrel.
Flames in the marsh. A setting sun.

*

Sib-sib, went the bird. *Sib-sib.*
'Is that a dunnock?'
I asked the twitcher as he passed,
'A siskin, a bunting, a chiff-chaff?'
He was dressed in green
like a man of the woods
and roped with long-range lenses.
Sib-sib, went the bird again. *Sib-sib.*
'There,' I said, 'listen,' and he did,
his ear tilted like a satellite dish,
but he couldn't tell me,
or wouldn't tell me,
and stepped away towards the hide
with a curt 'G'day'.
I raised my binocs
in hopes of a glimpse —
wing, tail, anything.
But the bird stayed hid
and its call faded
behind the reeds and the radio masts.
Sib-sib, sib-sib, sib-sib.

*

There's a hiss in the reeds, a shush in the surf.
Scrunch your heel in the sand and it whispers.
There's a secret, you know there's a secret.
But the shingle keeps it. The pebbles stay schtum.

*

The sea's all frills.
It flounces in
with a roll of eyes
and lift of underthings,
riding your way
on a roar of applause
till the flashbulbs go off
and it slows and stops,
turning back
with a lacy hem.

*

The wind-shaven bushes on the cliff edge
peer through the sea-fret like sentries
while daggered prows sneak up the beach.

*

The maltings, the saltings, the sandlings, the stone.
The fishmonger with scales on his arms.
The mirror-light of mudflats at dawn.

*

One year when we came down
a line of shells had been laid
from the water up to the shacks.

Not just shells but bones,
feathers, cuttlefish, claws,
anything bleached by the sea.

White as lime or cremation ash,
the line ran straight as a die
through flocks of seakale and pea.

The ghost road, we called it,
as though the dead had crawled
from the sea and left this trail

across the shingle to the reed-beds,
where at night if you listen hard
you can hear them plotting revenge.

*

The starfish on the foreshore.
The starling in the saltmarsh.
The starlight on the sea.

The firewood in the hearth-grate.
The fireflies in the reed-bed.
The firestorm in the surf.

*

The sandpipers run ahead
like thoughts we've not yet had,
their legs whirring like watch-cogs.

*

tideswell seaslap crabscrawl
windscut landslack sandsail

*

Slim ditches through the reeds,
a herd of Jerseys by the sluice,
and beyond, where the marsh gives out,
a combine with its dust cloud of wheat.

*

Campion, garlic, pea and kale,
and a scrubby goat willow in the marshes
and a stunted apple tree in the dunes.

*

How the river fretting in the marshes
would love to meet up with the sea.
But it sulks in scummy pools,
under the thumb of a shingle bank,
while the waves live it up, just yards away.

*

White sand, white bone, the skull of a catfish
and an oystercatcher's skeleton,
the wind through them like a piccolo.

Rebecca Perry

efore I left for the residency, I'd bought a very old, stained copy of a Pitman's Shorthand exercise book from Pages of Hackney. I took it with me to Aldeburgh and, after a few hours of sitting in the relative dark next to a bright orange heater that clicked off every minute or so, my hands became too cold to hold a pen or type with any speed. I took out the book and started flicking through it, struck instantly by the strangeness of the language used in the various exercises. The beach outside was approaching dark grey and a mist was hovering over the pebbles — it fitted perfectly with the bizarre, almost violent, world inside the book. I started selecting certain words and phrases and collaged them together to make something that felt, at least to me, like a narrative of sorts. I doubt the poem would have come together in any other place.

Phonograph

She was held by a rope
to a tall pole on the beach
and what a nightmarish thought
with the strong wind and the
smoky clouds. Some people,
like some animals,
are said to be sleepless,
which the sea never is
and not the mind, either.

Her knees bend and her
eyes close in forgetting —
there's always something.
She remembers that some of
the beasts at the sale
were tied by the nose to posts
and now it's too late help.
She would wish to make
the storm a calm if she had
the power to wish anything.

Last Sunday he said:
to be of use ought to be
the aim of our lives.
To look at the stars on a clear
evening is to be impressed
by their number and the
immensity of space. Lastly,

the masters of all, whoever
they are, are blessed to
possess wisdom many
ages older than ours.
They long, like ourselves,
to flash across space a signal
of life and fellowship.

Andrea Porter

came to Aldeburgh as a teenager in the 1960s and walked the beach with the family dog in an attempt to avoid sitting in tea rooms or eating sandwiches on the beach behind a windbreak whilst my parents read newspapers or dozed. Walking the beach alone became in my head then the height of sophisticated angst in keeping with the times; the Vietnam War, The Civil Rights movement in America, the pill, apartheid, nuclear testing, the Bay of Pigs, these all fed into a huge maelstrom of how the world was. I read Plath and Baudelaire, my back resting against a fishing boat, huddled up to the dog for warmth when the wind blew. I wanted to question how a life should be lived in a world that always seemed on the edge of tipping into some abyss.

Coming back to Aldeburgh many years later for the Poetry Festival brought back all those memories of trying to figure out how the world was and I realised I was still asking those same questions and still reading. This time around there were poets, live poets not the ones on a page, there were poets from around the world and I walked the beach with their words and sometimes with them. The world still has wars, huge injustices and inequalities and if anything the complexity of life on the planet of ours, both micro and macro has increased. The sea at Aldeburgh was important not just as a scenic backdrop to a festival but as a marker of what does not change. The sea is ceaseless in its nature, just as those questions are. How poets and artists ask or respond to those big questions is hopefully ceaseless too.

What We May Ask of the Sea

This shore has asked me questions each year.
How far does the third wave travel?
Is the sky measured by the length of a beach?
Is the horizon always a slow curve?

The answers have lain somewhere between
the North Sea and I and in the clumsy way I
scrambled to find a footing on heaped shingle,
using the wind and the driving rain as a prop.

Sometimes words are thrown back in my face
with that particular taste of salt and storms.
I have stood here alone and with others
in silence, waiting for that precise moment

that eases into ok. We are ok and the silence
holds all the words and that long listening,
something gulls can steal from our mouths
and drop like hag stones into the water.

No one sees ripples in the business of tides,
circles spreading from a point of impact,
yet one change in the way it all is makes
way for the possibility of moving an ocean.

Sue Rose

ldeburgh has been a spiritual home from home for me for years: as a forum for new voices (the ever-evolving annual poetry festival), as a trove of one-of-a-kind earrings (the quirky shops along Aldeburgh high street), and as a place where the sometimes bitter weather has always been mitigated by warm hospitality. It is also the site of Caroline Wiseman's home and gallery at the base of the Lookout, where I bought the mysterious print 'Idus Martiae', by photographer Bill Jackson, which now hangs in my home and which inspired this poem.

Blind Tides
(after Bill Jackson)

Braille under a photographer's soles,
the invisible beach is a book of stones
as he angles his camera in the cold
of night to catch each phase, a slow
shading, dun to indigo to waking light.
Past the horizon, the sea's blind tides
breathe, their frivolous surface miles
above those languid forms of life
that colour the deep, each a code
in bioluminescence to be read
as food or friend or foe.
Marine dark unfolds as his lens
waits for stories unattended,
translates time into abstract lines.

Anna Selby

I had looked at the tower longingly in previous years when at the Aldeburgh Poetry Festival. I arrived on a heavy winter day and wanted to live there forever. As I wrote, I thought of Dylan Thomas in his boat house jutting over the water. Snow had settled on the pebbles and I slept so close to the fire that I thought the blankets would catch. The sea was feral and I dreamt all night that it flooded in through the door and floated me down the street.

Death of the Fish March

White birds know which god to follow,
how to fake it, how to roll and whip their wings
with grief, a reincarnated chorus: wailers flailing
behind the pyre. Gulls flipping themselves over to grief,
a flurry of grief, grief the slow motoring
chug, grief the car kept ticking, grief shoving
grief out of the way for a glimpse, grief the white
handkerchiefs waving them off, grief the paper blown
from a burnt-out building,
grief the cold hand on your neck, grief
a flung back beak, grief the shriek
as they pass over, grief the loss as they move out of shot,
grief circling above as they get closer to the handing over of the dead,
always close enough to feel the breath rise
from the trawler, the last heat of the boat,
the shine of death as the offerings slip from the nets.
My grief wonders what my grandfather whistled,
what tune it was that made my grandmother follow.
Death does not wait for fisherwomen, they tug it to them
gasping, and stay with it until the end,
scrubbing the dead from their fingernails.
Only when they return with the bodies glinting,
can the procession begin.

Dunwich Burning

*'The burning' is a phrase used in north Norfolk to
describe phosphorescence*

My accomplice stumbles away out of colour,
then stops at the edge abruptly, as if the sea
were a window that appeared in his house.
The ship-like buildings of midnight mount behind us:
moonset fugitives, two smugglers wading into our silence.
We swim above a town they say sunk beneath us.
If the tide were low enough, the wind
would rush through the bell towers. I turn back,
skin crackling and could cry or sing,
shaking constellations from my hands. Stars slip
off my fingers, like scales from a fisherwoman's knife.
We lay each other out in wet sand.
The waves extinguish themselves,
tug and resist bare feet, bare shins, bare skin.
And yes, the town might never have existed,
but even if you imagine it, it will lie
somewhere there before you. The legend
is still hauled from the depths, and there are hours
of fire left, and the sea is sinking in.

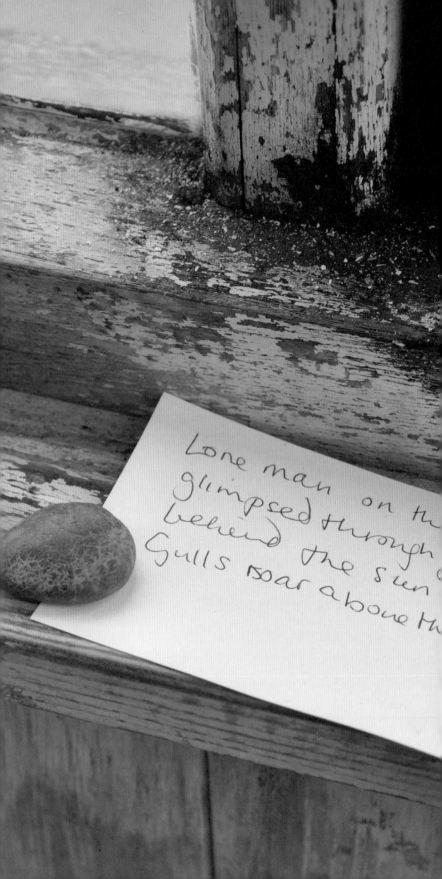

Gemma Seltzer

I love cities: the roaring rush of them, with their chaotic crowds and buildings that fill the skyline. So finding myself wrapped in blankets during the early hours of a cold February day, listening to the pause between waves crashing, staring from the Lookout into the black sky, was a new experience. I wrote as one by one the flashing lights on the horizon disappeared. I wrote as shadows turned into shingles. I wrote about the sunrise, dog walkers, candles, stairways, the table, a chair, pencils. I wrote because I might have been afraid of the quiet. I wrote to address, and claim, everything I saw as morning arrived. It was glorious.

Thank you to Julia Bird for inviting a few of us writers to stay in the Lookout and share our words on Aldeburgh beach. And heartfelt thanks to Caroline and Francis for opening their home to me with such hospitality.

Aldeburgh beach in early morning light

Lookout
Lady tower, stairwell ribbons trailing your shoulder, watching the
sea's paper rustle dance. I crouch to read the language of your
wooden floorboards, prickled with paint. The scaffolding net upstairs
casts a shade of bottle green, so the sun rises in orange-green, the
clouds roll white-green and a woman with a leaping dog has cheeks
flushed red-green. Below, your belly hiccups forwards, as only an
undone trouser belt might allow. And outside? Where there were
four lights in the distance, there is now one.

Sea
Beneath a dirty white sky, you shuffle to shore, wet tongue licking
shingles, toothpaste foaming around your mouth. When I think
you have perfected your even rolling waves, marking the beach
with your furthest stretch, you take a breath and grope further still.
Sea, you play. Sea, I play too. I shed my shoes and sprint into your
watery chest.

Shingle
Regal in plumes of black, capes of white, marble crowns. You
embrace polystyrene tubing, garden hoses, cigarette butts with
weathered fingers. Except for the crunch and sink of walking figures
on your shoulders, that way you can be calm, like nothing else can
be calm. You are dutiful, if nothing else, shingles.

Sky
Blue hum, spread overhead, blue hum. A backdrop to a burst of
cumulus. I sit in blue but I do not know I do. Below is not you, the
clouds are not you, the lighthouse is not you, beach and sea not.
Sunrays like perforated paper edges. Deep blue to light blue. You're
the kind who rages at the injustice of the, sadness of the, fear of the.
And then is serene and soars through to do lists and with many ticks.

Sun
Shy baby with golden hair. Child afraid of bawling gulls. Teenager
hiking Himalayan tracks and exploring Australian coasts and
looping Fijian flowers around your neck. You returned to the sky
having lived and deciding how you would live. As an adult, you are
able to charm the horizon. You float above now, arms around white
fluffs, grinning light.

Penelope Shuttle

Every time I came to Aldeburgh for the Poetry Festival, I'd walk on the beach and wish I could climb to the top of the South Lookout tower. So I was delighted when the opportunity arose for poets to sign up for an hour in the tower, and to write about it. It was a rainy blowy morning when I climbed up the rickety staircase into the bare wooden chamber room at the very top of the tower. The sea was raging away to itself in great grey billows, the rain kept coming and going in frets and skirmishes, and fleeting bits of sunlight shot across the sky. I relished the sense of being up in the sky, where the weather comes from, and this sense of elemental exhilaration is what, several years later, I recall. I'd love to go back and climb that tower again, spend an hour in meditation on sea and sky, rain, sun, and the whaleback hump of the shingle beach...

Moth and Rain

South Lookout tower, Aldeburgh

Remains of a moth
white-brindle wings

spread in death-flight
on the window sill

in the leaky lookout
plus a cache of dopey flies

damp tree house without a tree
crow's nest without a ship

from up here
the world is nipped-back

to Thorpeness
a mile to the left

and a shrug of a mile
to the right... somewhere else

Across a sweep
of rain-clean shingle —

grey sea   grey sky

waves tend their surf
to sound of seagull psalms

sky strong as an ox
moving its big clouds
from stem to stern

sea interlude performed
for all listeners

lookout's watcher
counting

slow raindrops
peppering the old floorboards

sighting the anglers
along the strandline

with their dogged little tents
The winds lie low

letting clouds and rain
take the rap

Strokes of silver light
to southward

and when the sun warms
the lookout tower

those darn flies wake up
and cuss.

George Szirtes

he poem 'Howard Hodgkin Considers the Moon' was written as part of a collaboration between The London Magazine and Caroline Wiseman, who invited poets to respond to works of art in her collection. When Caroline moved to Aldeburgh, I read there on one occasion with other poets brought along by Tom Corbett. I had been familiar with the festival of course and read and attended a good many times. So Aldeburgh is a beautiful, resonant place, full of memories.

Howard Hodgkin Considers the Moon

When it comes to me, green, through the green window
it is not green but brown. When it enters the back
of the eyes it is not brown but black with a faint afterglow.
When I wake in the night, once again it is black,
then swells into a kind of gold or foxed yellow.

When the moon rises, that which is cold freezes
and creeps under the nails with a peculiar noise
I can't quite identify. When, eventually, it squeezes
through the double glazing it is a blend of alloys
passing through the usual predictable phases:

now full, then mildly dented like an old football,
cut sharp in the middle, a slice of lemon,
the merest sliver of ice left on the floor, a small
dense patch of nothing. But who are these women
sitting immobile, patient in the hall?

I feel their cold. Their manners are the politesse
of death, their small talk is of moons waning.
I watch them as they rise and dress
in little black numbers. Their stars hang
in the cupboard. The moon waits on the terrace.

Surge

As the wind dies down
the sea picks up. So land falls
and water rises.

And the brittle shore
breaks, much as the sea can break,
constantly broken.

We are disasters
on the edge of our own shores,
dreaming and woken.

Nothing permanent
about us. If sea can break
so can shore and cliff.

The thought of the sea
is a form of rising. Sky
over high water.

The church with its hymns.
The sailors with their shanties.
Sand with its shifting.

In every cadence
the certainty of water,
the howling of wind.

The tide closing in
on the throat. The billowing.
The wretched dark cloud.

We dream beginnings
and endings. Everything moves
to its own cadence.

The long run is now.
The sea constantly rolling
into the present.

Harriet Tarlo

y experience of the Lookout tower was a short collaborative residency with artist Judith Tucker in October 2015 entitled *Seeing Double*. We went out each day at dawn and dusk at approximately 6am and 6pm to walk the shore away from and back to the tower. We were interested in exploring the relation of the very particular architecture of the vertical tower in contrast to the horizontal shingle beach and in the idea of looking out and looking back in, of inside and outside, which we did. However, we work by remaining open to what we see and sense around us. The changing sound and colour of the stones, sea and sky also became important to me on the walks, as well as the found objects (fish hooks, chip forks, crab claws) becoming abstract or 'natural' again, as the sea and stones eroded them. The most extraordinary find was Hester's message in a bottle which was returned to the sea at the end of the residency. I also talked to people on the beach and visited the friendly library and museum to do a little local research.

Judith made drawings and I wrote a sequence (part of which is published here) and one or two individual poems about found objects on the beach and the different tower rooms. Judith's drawings focused on the framing of the tower windows, as I had expected my poems to do, but, to my surprise, this wave form was insistently imposed itself on my words, so I went with it, focusing on shape and line-endings to make these open-form poems. The poems and drawings were exhibited together on the walls inside the tower and projected in fragmentary form on to the outside wall. I also read the poems aloud on a public walk at the end of the residency. Caroline Wiseman, with her badly broken leg in a cast, staggered determinedly over the road to the tower for the event and sat like a presiding white witch by the fire and amongst candles, sending us out and welcoming us back.

from **Dawn Dusk Dawn**

Dawn 1

Gulls

circle greys

2 verticals cross stones

street lamps mark town to ocean

pick out white wave line end and up, seeming stopped

by ridges' *fulls* and *slashes*, made by sea,

marked by feet, each step

dappling the

pattern

Light

comes in, flecks

out whiter shingles,

coloured crenellations, morning

growing through town windows, waking to

grey-brown sea, boat, rope

net, bottle, tub tangle

feather stone

bend

Gold

enters flint

blue in rope, lighter still

as three fly close and low over

ocean, flag flaps outside palest green Brudenell

pink-orange opens out new space

in white-grey

sky

Found

in a weighted

bottle, green letters

on rough pink paper, fading out orange:

Rest in Peace

Beautiful Emily

Missed and

loved always

all my love

Hester
x

Blood

balloon, deflating

heart or organ quivers

and bobs, string caught straining

under stones, not rising. Cloud closes grey

silver over again, over all our

loud steps back to

tower and

town

Dusk 1

Six

brings sun

just before we slow

spin from it, catching the white in

a bird's bone, sea holly silver, Sizewell's bubble

long lines of scoter streaking across

pink-grey layers of sky

flicking back from

windows

Tonight

the Brudenell

is blue, not green

caught in gold from beyond, behind

the town where saltmarsh, once grassland, sets sun's end.

Sky pales as sea darkens. Fishermen, their backs

to the ocean, twist and throw

their bodies round,

send out

a line

In last light a late yellow poppy, horned pods sent up

crooked to split over shingle, looks back from

Slaughden where they opened

their doors front and back

and let the sea

wash in

'till it came

too many times

took the Mariners' Arms

Dovey Pettit's laundry at Fort Green

the Shepherd's place, even the hazard house gone

Hester thought she could talk to

the sea and it might listen under the shingle

even answer. *There is no sea like the Aldeburgh sea*

Fitzgerald wrote, *it talks to me.* We hear

our own voices back, do we?

Siriol Troup

ust a view — let's not make a big thing of it — a view
through a hotel window of sea, nothing but sea, grey sea,
half-set half-wet abstraction corrugated with apparently
motionless peaks working through light and its absence towards
a view of sea I'd like to frame, absolute all-at-sea-ness I try to
tether to concrete or icing, elephant hide or turtle neck or the
loose flag between index finger and thumb staking claim to
the view I never quite get, but end up diving into like a splash
of paint.

Fee-fi-fo-fum
Martello Tower, Aldeburgh

Time was when Albion trembled
in the corner of a world
where Paris was the centre.

Napoleon stood on his pride.
Six centuries of insults to avenge!
Songs were written, medals fired —
Descente en Angleterre
by raft, balloon or subaquatic tunnel.
The Bayeux Tapestry had shown the way.
Impossible did not exist in French!

John Bull boiled and fumed.
No pocket Hannibal
or seven-league Puss-in-Boots
could scoff his fine plum-pudding!
British design must hold the fort.
Martello Towers along the coast
would give that Boney ass
a pretty peppering.

Across the ditch
flat-bottomed boats were spoiling
for a fight. Sauce whets the appetite —
invasion would require
three hundred thousand
pints of brandy.

But Aldeburgh's tower —
a four-leaf clover —
shaped our pudding's luck.
No need for musket fire or cannonades
or whacks of British pluck:
before the final bricks were laid
L'Armée des Côtes de l'Océan stood down.
The Tiddy Doll had lost his bite,
the Shuttlecock his crown.

Robert Vas Dias

C aroline first introduced my wife Maggie and me to the work of Howard Hodgkin. His carborundum colour etching 'Snow' beguiled us and was the beginning of our fascination with with his work and that of other modern and contemporary British artists, including Maggi Hambling whom we first met at Caroline's house in Stockwell. Much later Hambling made a charcoal portrait of me.

In that house-cum-gallery I saw Hodgkin's colour etching 'Realism', which provoked 'Conjugal Love Poem'. I started this poem by turning the platitude "Nothing is as it seems" on its head, because I felt Hodgkin was being playfully ironical by calling his painting 'Realism'. What is real, he appeared to be saying, is what I paint it as being, what the painting calls up emotionally. I call this poem 'Conjugal Love Poem' because two people in a long-lasting and close relationship may accept diversity as contributing to rather than detracting from their affinity, which is perhaps not the conventional idea of conjugal love. The traditional regularity of the form, a villanelle, does not accord with what the poem is saying, another instance of the paradox I see in the painting.

I took part in Caroline's Aldeburgh Art festival in May 2011, and when walking along the beach I came across Hambling's scallop sculpture in homage to Benjamin Britten; a child was sitting in it looking out to a grey sea. Did she hear in the sea's ceaseless surge "those voices that will not be drowned"?

Conjugal Love Poem

What you see is not the way I see.
    What I see is just the ways things are,
        Everything is always as it seems.

What colour are these trousers?
    You say they're grey, I say they're green,
        What you see is not the way I see.

Whether blue or black, rough or smooth,
    Against the grain or uniform,
        Everything is always as it seems.

Let's shelve our books alphabetically.
    No, you say, by size for harmony.
        What you see is not the way I see.

We've lived together, you and I, for years
    Of harmonious disparity, for
        Everything is always as it seems,

And that's the way I'd rather have it.
    Let's embrace our incongruity. Or not:
        What you see is not the way I see.
        Everything is always as it seems.

Tamar Yoseloff

I arrived in Aldeburgh for my residency, ready to write my great 'sea poem', but then encountered the dilemma that many poets before me have faced: how do you write about the sea when Arnold, Masefield, Stevens have all done it before you, and their words are tumbling around in your head? I'd brought some 'inspirational' books with me, intending to create a reading area for visitors to the Lookout during the weekend. I had natural history guides, Sebald, Mabey, Ewart Evans, Blythe, and some poets, including W S Graham. Not that Graham had anything to do with Suffolk, but his vision of the sea, from his vantage points of both Scotland and Cornwall, is extraordinary. And, as it happens, he also writes about the difficulty of language, how impossible it is to say what you need to say with only our common vocabulary. I didn't set out to write about Graham — my first poems composed in the little writing room that once belonged to Laurens van der Post were about gulls, rain (included here) and rust. But a conversation about Graham I'd had with Francis the first night, particularly his incredible poem, 'The Thermal Stair' — a tribute to his late friend, the landscape painter Peter Lanyon — stuck in my head. My tribute to Graham, asking his assistance with my challenging sea poem, came on the third day. Poets sometimes have personal favourites: poems that mean more to them than others, possibly because the occasion or location of writing is so important. If I have a favourite of all my poems, it is this one, composed in that magical place, looking out from my post in the tower through a rain-smeared window at the grey sea.

A Letter to WS Graham

Sydney — if I may call you Sydney — because I feel
you have been speaking to me all this time,
in the complex, common tongue you attempted
to decipher. And I've been listening, here
by the sea you said was listening. It is a space,
the sea, like all the other spaces you tried to
(de)construct, it is a poem that finds its turn
along the shoreline; a lament, a plain-
tive voice, like the mother of a drowned child.

The light is variable, and I write to hold it against
the shadows. It's all we can ever do — try to hold
a moment disappearing even as we whisper its name
and place it in the light. Break here, stop
your difficult glances and cantankerous rambles.
Tell me
      how to say something about the sea
that hasn't been said in thousands of words,
stumbling across the page like drunks, none of them
up to the job. The job is love, you said,
that's why we stretch ourselves into a thousand
suffering shapes, like Hilton's nudes or Lanyon's thermals.
You made words of their colours, made words
for the sea that fancies itself a metaphor, too pretty
and brutal for simple truth.
                 Tell me
now that your words are done, how to keep going on.
The coast stretches too far for me to see,
but you're ahead, in a lonely place (we make our own,
you said); from there you must be able to see us all,
lighting lamps with our voices.

You are the lighthouse now, beaming
and winking, gently guiding us away
from the treacherous rocks.

The rain

arrives and is queen, her great ermine of cloud
issuing the rule of water. We obey her,
worship by raising bright canopies.

Her reign is long and prosperous in the greening
of the land, the flowing of rivers.
We are anointed, cleansed.

The sky carries her dark warnings, her weapons;
the earth releases its hidden subjects,
stems blossoming in her name.

She declaims against the frivolous sun; no good
can come in a world at play. We must suffer
and love it. We must work for joy.

Biographies

Daphne Astor is a poet, artist and farmer living and working in East Anglia. She was born in New York City into a family deeply embedded in the arts and grew up moving continually between NYC, the Blue Ridge Mountains in Virginia, and New Mexico. After receiving a BA from NYU Film School she left the USA to work in various locations in Asia for two years then moved her studio to Paris in 1977 – she settled in East Anglia soon after. She is currently on the board of The Poetry School, C4RD and she is the curator for Poetry in Aldeburgh 2016.

Anne Berkeley edited Rebecca Elson's posthumous first collection, *A Responsibility to Awe* (Carcanet) and the poetry journal *Seam*. She has performed widely with the poetry ensemble The Joy of Six. Her first collection, *The Men from Praga* (Salt), was shortlisted for the Seamus Heaney Centre Prize in 2010.

Simon Barraclough is a poet, writer, performer and editor based in London. His poetry collections are *Los Alamos Mon Amour* (2008), *Bonjour Tetris* (2010), *Neptune Blue* (2011), *Psycho Poetica* (as editor, 2012), *The Debris Field: Salvaging the Titanic in Word, Sound and Image* (with Isobel Dixon and Chris McCabe, 2013), *Laboratorio: Poems from the Mullard Space Science Laboratory* (as editor, 2015) and *Sunspots* (2015).

Julia Bird grew up in Gloucestershire and now lives in London where she is Creative Director of the Poetry School, and also works as an independent live literature producer. Her collections *Hannah and the Monk* (2008) and *Twenty-four Seven Blossom* (2013) are published by Salt.

Matthew Caley's *Thirst* (Slow Dancer, 1999) was nominated for the Forward Prize for Best First Collection. He has read his work in low dives and grand halls – from the National Portrait Gallery to the Gypsy Hill Tavern; Morden Tower to the South Bank's 'The Rest Is Noise' festival; from The Betsey Trotwood in Farringdon to Alchemy in Prague; from Shakespeare's Globe to a puppet theatre in Novi Sad, Serbia. He has published four more collections since his debut, the latest being *Rake* (Bloodaxe, 2016).

Catherine Coldstream lives in Oxford where she studied and now teaches theology. She has completed an MA in Creative Non-Fiction at UEA and is currently a doctoral candidate at Goldsmiths, where she studies Creative Writing with Blake Morrison. Several of her poems and short stories have been placed in competitions, and extracts of her memoir and other writings published in anthologies. She is keen string player, and a member of the Oxford String Quartet.

Joey Connolly lives in London, where he is the manager of the Poetry Book Fair. His work has appeared in publications including *The Poetry Review*, *Poetry London*, *The Sunday Times* and *Best British Poetry 2014* (Salt), as well as on BBC Radio 4. He received an Eric Gregory award in 2012, and his first collection, *Long Pass*, is forthcoming from Carcanet in 2017.

Claire Crowther has published three full poetry collections; the first, *Stretch of Closures*, was shortlisted for the Aldeburgh prize. She has also published four pamphlets; her most recent is *Bare George*, written during her residency at the Royal Mint museum. Her poems have appeared in such journals as the *London Review of Books*, *New Statesman* and *Times Literary Supplement*. She reviews poetry for *Poetry London*, *London Magazine* and other journals.

Tim Cumming's first collection, *The Miniature Estate*, was published in 1991, and subsequent books include *Apocalypso*, *Contact Print*, *The Rumour* and *The Rapture*. *Etruscan Miniatures* (2012) and *Rebel Angels in the Mind Shop* (2015) were published by Pitt Street Poetry, Australia. He has made a series of acclaimed film poems and exhibited poems and paintings at Sladers Yard gallery in Dorset. His work has appeared in three editions of *The Forward Book of Poetry*, its 2004 Best of the Decade anthology, and the Bloodaxe Books 2010 anthology, *Identity Parade*.

Rebecca Farmer is in her final year of a creative writing PhD at Goldsmiths where she is researching the later works of Louis MacNeice. Her debut pamphlet, *Not Really*, was a winner of the 2014 Poetry Business Pamphlet Prize judged by Carol Ann Duffy. In 2016 she was one of four writers to be awarded Writer in Residence at Gladstone's Library. Her poems have been widely published in magazines including *The Poetry Review*, *The London Magazine*, *The Warwick Review* and *The North*.

Annie Freud is a poet and artist. Her first collection, *The Best Man That Ever Was* (Picador 2007), was a Poetry Book Society recommendation and was awarded The Dimplex Prize for New Writing. *The Mirabelles* (Picador 2010), her second collection, was a Poetry Book Society Choice and was short-listed for the TS Eliot Prize. Her third collection, *The Remains*, was published in 2015. She was named by the Poetry Book Society as one of the Next Generation Poets 2014.

Anne-Marie Fyfe's fifth poetry collection is *House of Small Absences* (Seren Books, 2015). Born in Cushendall, County Antrim, Anne-Marie lives in London where she works as an arts organiser. She has run Coffee-House Poetry's readings and classes at London's Troubadour since 1997, is Poetry Co-ordinator for the annual John Hewitt International Summer School in Armagh City, and is a former chair of the UK's Poetry Society. annemariefyfe.com

Rody Gorman was born in Dublin in 1960 and lives on the Isle of Skye in Scotland. He has published 15 collections in English, Irish and Scottish Gaelic. He has worked in residencies at the University of Manitoba, Sabhal Mòr Ostaig at the University of Highlands and Islands, University College Cork and PROGR in Berne. He edits the annual Gaelic anthology *An Guth*.

Ian Griffiths was born and grew up in Swansea, birthplace of the poet Dylan Thomas, whose work inspired his love of poetry and influenced some of his own later work. He moved to Suffolk forty years ago and is a former chairman of Suffolk Poetry Society. He is currently a committee member of the new Poetry In Aldeburgh festival. He has performed his work throughout the UK and the USA, has published several of his poems, and his first collection, entitled *Conversations with Birds*, is to be released later in 2016.

Michael Horovitz founded New Departures publications and Live New Departures in 1959, Jazz Poetry SuperJams in 1970 and the Poetry Olympics festivals in 1980. He has produced some 50 books of poetry and prose including *A New Waste Land* and *Wordsounds & Sightlines* as well as various recordings. Recent collaborations with musicians resulted in two Jazz Poetry SuperJam records, an LP and single from Gearbox Records featuring Damon Albarn, Graham Coxon and Paul Weller. Allen Ginsberg characterised him as a "Popular, experienced, experimental, New Jerusalem, Jazz Generation, Sensitive Bard". poetryolympics.com

Pamela Johnson's poems appear in magazines and anthologies. She has published two novels, *Under Construction* and *Deep Blue Silence*, with Sceptre. Her third, *Taking In Water*, supported by an Arts Council Writers' Award, was published in 2016 by Blue Door Press. She has worked as an independent critic and curator; her writing on contemporary visual art and craft has appeared in journals, broadsheets and gallery publications. She's curated national touring exhibitions and reviewed for BBC Radio 4's *Kaleidoscope* and *Front Row*. She is currently working on her fourth novel and first poetry collection, runs the website Words Unlimited and teaches on the MA in Creative and Life Writing at Goldsmiths.

Gerry Loose is a poet and artist who works primarily with subjects from the natural world, most specifically with plants, as well as the world of geo-politics. His work is found inscribed and created in parks, botanic gardens, natural landscapes, galleries and on the page. Recent commissioned exhibitions are Sylva Caledonia in Summerhall, Edinburgh (Edinburgh Science Festival), and Glas, at Aldeburgh and Snape Maltings (both 2015). Recent publications include *fault line* (Vagabond Voices) and *An Oakwoods Almanac* (Shearsman).

Ian McMillan was born in 1956 and has been a freelance writer, performer and broadcaster since 1981. He's written poems, stories and plays for radio and the stage and he currently presents BBC Radio 3's cabaret of the word, *The Verb*. His latest collection of poems is *To Fold The Evening Star* from Carcanet.

Leanne Moden is a poet from Norfolk, now living in Nottingham. She has performed all around the UK, including events at the Royal Albert Hall, Manchester University and Trinity College Cambridge, and festivals including Aldeburgh Poetry Festival, Cambridge Festival of Ideas and Bestival on the Isle of Wight. As Fenland Poet Laureate, she founded the Fen Speak open mic nights and curated the *Glass Cases and Curios* anthology. She hosts the Crosswords open mic in Nottingham and is part of the DIY Poets collective. Her pamphlet *Liaisons* was published by Stewed Rhubarb Press in 2015.

Blake Morrison is a poet, novelist, librettist and the author of two bestselling memoirs, *And When Did You Last See Your Father?* and *Things My Mother Never Told Me*. He has published studies of The Movement and Seamus Heaney, and he edited the landmark anthology *Penguin Book of Contemporary British Poetry* with Andrew Motion. His poetry collections include *Dark Glasses*, *The Ballad of the Yorkshire Ripper* and *A Discoverie of Witches*. His latest publications are a pamphlet, *This Poem...* (2013) and the collection *Shingle Street* (2015). He is Professor of Creative and Life Writing at Goldsmiths.

Rebecca Perry's first full collection, *Beauty/Beauty* (Bloodaxe, 2015), was a Poetry Book Society Recommendation, and shortlisted for the Fenton Aldeburgh Prize for Best First Collection, The Seamus Heaney Centre Prize and the TS Eliot Prize. Rebecca is co-editor of the online journal *Poems in Which* and lives in London.

Andrea Porter's poems have been included in the *Forward Book of Poetry* and *Poetry of the Decade*, both published by Faber. A narrative sequence of poems ('Bubble') was adapted for BBC Radio 4. Her debut collection was *A Season of Small Insanities* (Salt). Her last book, *House of the Deaf Man* (Gatehouse), is a collaborative book with the award winning artist Tom de Freston in response to the 'Black Paintings' of Francisco Goya, which was launched at the Lookout. She has read at the Aldeburgh Poetry Festival twice, as a member of The Joy of Six and as an individual.

Sue Rose lives in Kent and works as a literary translator. Her debut collection of poetry, *From the Dark Room*, was published by Cinnamon Press in 2011. In 2014, she brought out *Heart Archives*, a chapbook of sonnets and photos, with Hercules Editions, and her second collection, *The Cost of Keys*, was also published by Cinnamon Press. She won the Troubadour Poetry Prize in 2009 and the Canterbury Festival Poet of the Year Competition in 2008.

Anna Selby's poems often explore our connection with water, the natural world and are influenced by contemporary poetry from Eastern Europe. She has been listed as one of five poets to watch by *The Huffington Post*, voted as a top ten cultural innovator working in publishing and writing by *Time Out*. Her pamphlet, *The Burning*, was published in 2013 and her work has been featured in *Magma*, *The Rialto* and the anthology *Ghost of Gone Birds* (Bloomsbury). Her poetry-dance collaborations have been shortlisted for The Oxford Samuel Beckett Theatre Trust Award, featured on the BBC Two's *The Culture Show* and are touring nationally.

Gemma Seltzer is a writer working online, live and in print. Her projects include improvised text and dance piece *Performing Small Spaces* (2014), a year of city explorations with a photographer in *5am London* (2012) and daily fiction blog *Speak to Strangers* (2009) based on random interactions with Londoners, published as a book by Penned in the Margins. Gemma has been writer-in-residence for the Olympic torch relay and Tate Modern, and has presented her work on BBC radio and at the Venice Biennale. She also runs Write & Shine, early morning writing classes in peaceful locations. gemmaseltzer.co.uk

Penelope Shuttle has lived in Cornwall since 1970. She is a tutor and mentor for a number of organisations, including The Poetry School. *Heath* was published by Nine Arches Press in July 2016, and a pamphlet, *Four Portions of Everything on the Menu for M'sieur Monet!*, was published by Indigo Dreams in August 2016. Her twelfth collection, *Will You Walk a Little Faster?*, will be published in May 2017 by Bloodaxe Books.

George Szirtes is a poet, translator and author of many books. He won the TS Eliot Prize for *Reel* in 2004 and his two subsequent books were also shortlisted. His recent publications are *Mapping the Delta* (Bloodaxe, 2016) and *56*, co-written with Carol Watts (Arc, 2016).

Harriet Tarlo is a poet, academic and Reader in Creative Writing at Sheffield Hallam University. Publications include *Poems 2004–2014* and *Poems 1990–2003* (Shearsman); *Nab* (etruscan, 2005) and, with Judith Tucker, *Sound Unseen and Behind Land* (Wild Pansy, 2013 and 2015). She edited *The Ground Aslant: An Anthology of Radical Landscape Poetry* (Shearsman, 2011). Her collaborative work with Tucker has been shown at many galleries, including Musée de Moulages, Lyon, 2013; Southampton City Art Gallery 2013–14; and the New Hall College Art Collection, Cambridge, 2015.

Siriol Troup's collection *Beneath the Rime* is published by Shearsman. Her poems can be found in or are forthcoming from *Magma*, *The Poetry Review*, *Modern Poetry in Translation* and *PN Review*. She is currently working on a translation into verse of Goethe's *Italian Journey* and has just completed her third collection.

Robert Vas Dias, an Anglo-American resident in London, has published twelve collections in the UK and USA, the most recent of which is *Arrivals & Departures: Prose Poems* (Shearsman, 2014). A new collaborative book with British artist Julia Farrer, *Black Book*, will appear in autumn 2016. His poetry and criticism have appeared in over 100 magazines, journals and anthologies. He has recently published papers on the prose poem and on the American poets Paul Blackburn and Jackson Mac Low. robertvasdias.com

Vanessa Vie was born in Aviles, Asturias, Northern Spain. In 2012, she met Michael Horovitz, whose inspiration, encouragement and collaboration (appearing in Michael's Jazz/Poetry SuperJams and sundry national and international musical, literary and multi-cultural festivals), has been crucial to her artistic development. They are currently assembling their first music, song and wordsounds CD and illustrated book, under the working title of *Lyrical Soulmates*. Her poetry and art have been published in small magazines and pamphlets. She has been the lead singer-songwriter of two alternative rock bands, Ithaca (1997) and Rockatron (2005), also playing guitar and harmonica. vanessavie.co.uk

Tamar Yoseloff's fifth collection, *A Formula for Night: New and Selected Poems*, was published by Seren in 2015. She is also the author of *Formerly*, a chapbook with photographs by Vici MacDonald (Hercules Editions, 2012), shortlisted for the Ted Hughes Award; two collaborative editions with the artist Linda Karshan; and a book with the artist David Harker. She lives in London, where she is a tutor in creative writing, and in Suffolk, where she has a cottage in Blaxhall, the village immortalised by George Ewart Evans in his book, *Ask the Fellows Who Cut the Hay*. tamaryoseloff.com

Acknowledgements

Julia Bird's poem 'The Boast' was originally published in *Twenty-four Seven Blossom* (Salt, 2013)

Joey Connolly's poem 'Themselves' was originally published in *New Poetries VI* (Carcanet, 2015) and is copyrighted and reprinted here by kind permission of Carcanet Press Ltd, Manchester, UK

Annie Freud's poem 'Head of a Woman' was originally published in *The Mirabelles* (Picador, 2010) and is reproduced with permission of Pan Macmillan via PLSclear

Michael Horovitz's poem 'Sea Song' was originally published in *Wordsounds and Sightlines* (New Departures, 2001)

Gerry Loose's poems were originally commissioned by The Poetry Trust for the 2015 Aldeburgh Poetry Festival

Ian Griffiths's poem 'The Light Keeper's Daughter' was originally published in the Winter/Spring 2016 edition of *The Seventh Quarry Swansea Poetry Magazine*, Issue 23

Leanne Moden's poem 'Lighter', was written as part of a residency with Fran Crowe for her Museum of Beyond exhibition and was originally published on the website museumofbeyond.org

Blake Morrison's poem 'Flotsam' was originally published in *Shingle Street* (Chatto & Windus, 2015) and is reproduced by permission of The Random House Group Ltd

Rebecca Perry's poem 'Phonograph' was originally published in *Beauty/Beauty* (Bloodaxe, 2015)

Anna Selby's poems 'Death of the Fish March' and 'Dunwich Burning' were originally published in *The Burning* (Salt New Voices, 2013)

George Szirtes's poem 'Howard Hodgkin Considers the Moon' was originally published in *The Burning of the Books* (Bloodaxe, 2009)

Robert Vas Dias's poem 'Conjugal Love Poem' was originally published in *Still • Life, and Other Poems of Art and Artifice* (Exeter: Shearsman Books, 2010)

Tamar Yoseloff's poem 'A Letter to WS Graham' was originally published in *A Formula for Night: New and Selected Poems* (Seren, 2015)